Loose in Far-away Places

Loose in Far-away Places

Ann Herlong-Bodman

Press 53
Winston-Salem

Press 53, LLC
PO Box 30314
Winston-Salem, NC 27130

First Edition

Copyright © 2017 by Ann Herlong-Bodman

All rights reserved, including the right of reproduction in whole or in part in any form except in the case of brief quotations embodied in critical articles or reviews. For permission, contact publisher at editor@Press53.com, or at the address above.

Cover design by Kevin Morgan Watson

Cover photograph, "Hope Floats," copyright © 2014 by Dawn D. Surratt, used by permission of the artist.

Author photo by Barbara Lasher

Library of Congress Control Number 2017954780

Printed on acid-free paper
ISBN 978-1-941209-62-2

Over the great windy waters, and over the clear-crested summit,
Unto the sun and the sky, and into the perfecter earth,
Come, let us go . . .

—Arthur Hugh Clough, "Amour De Voyage, Canto 1"

. . . destinations . . . call to us
from a secret place within ourselves . . .

—Richard Bode, *First You Have to Row a Little Boat*

Grateful acknowledgment is made to the editors of the following publications in which these poems first appeared, sometimes with different titles and forms.

Atlanta Review: "The Art of Shucking an Oyster"
Cold Mountain Review: "Woman on a Hill," "Taking Flight"
The Cortland Review: "Found in Translation"
Fall Lines 2015: "Is there no escape" as "Island Time"
Iodine Poetry Journal: "Three Days Out, Somewhere in Middle America"
Kakalak, Anthology of Carolina Poets: "Breaking Bread with a Stranger," "The Return" as "Desert Woman," "Woman with Gold in Her Hair"
Main Street Rag: "Fennel"
The Poetry Society of South Carolina Yearbook: "Sailing Single-Handed" as "Fancying I've Learned Something about Sailing," DuBose and Dorothy Heyward Society Prize; "History 101," William Gilmore Simms Prize; "Trouble Is" as "At Midnight," Jeanne Crandall Broulik Memorial Prize; "Tabitha's Third Birthday," Carrie Allen McCray Prize
The South Carolina Review: "Instructions for the Tourist," "On Watch" as "Sailing West, Night Watch"
South 85 Journal: "Be Careful What You Wish For"
Southern Women Review: "During a Visit to Bosque Redondo"
Women Arts Quarterly Review: "It's the Lure" as "The Question of When"

"Be Careful What You Wish For" was nominated for the Best of the Net 2015 Anthology and named finalist in the 2014 Prime Number Magazine Award for Poetry.

"On Visiting the Site of a Massacre," as "When the Song Was Over, There Was Blood," was named finalist in the 2014 Prime Number Magazine Award for Poetry.

A special thank you to the South Carolina Poetry Initiative for choosing this manuscript runner-up in its 2009 South Carolina Poetry Book Prize contest, the 2015 Crab Orchard Series in the Open Competition Poetry Award for selecting the manuscript a semi-finalist, and The Word Works for naming the manuscript a 2015 semi-finalist for the Washington Prize.

Some poems were first published in the chapbook *Pulled Out of Sleep* (Pudding House Press, 2010).

Contents

Introduction by Susan Laughter Meyers   xi

ONE
Trouble is   3
It's the lure   4
Fennel   5
On Watch   6
Woman on a Hill   7
Found in Translation   8
Looking for King Midas   9
Taking Flight   11

TWO
Suite to the Sirens   15
The Art of Shucking an Oyster   23
Over bridges and great spans   25
Future Perfect   26
And I tell them   27
Gran's Funeral   28
Third Birthday   30
Morning Glory   31
Dolphin   32
On Visiting the Site of the Massacre   33
Be Careful What You Wish For   34

THREE
Three Days Out, Somewhere in Middle America   37
During a Visit to Bosque Redondo   39
At Rushmore   40
Nobody Knows the Trouble   41
The Return   42
Woman with Gold in Her Hair   43
Standing at the Rio Grande Gorge   44
Prisoner of Earth   45
A Summer Afternoon in Santa Fe   46
White people like me   47

FOUR

Epiphany	51
Passing Through	53
Is there no escape	54
Instructions for the Tourist	55
History 101	58
Raising Two Glasses	59
Breaking Bread with a Stranger	60
It's the Journey That Counts	61
Sailing Single-Handed	62
Notes	65
Acknowlegments	67
Author biography	69
Cover artist biography	71

Introduction
by Susan Laughter Meyers

"I'm shifting by degree," we hear in the opening poem of Ann Herlong-Bodman's *Loose in Far-away Places,* a collection filled with the wondrous vision of what it's like to journey—alone—away from the familiar. This bold and adventurous poet must have surprised even herself when one day she left her predictably safe landlubber life to venture seaward, on her own—to the unpredictable and the new. First, there's the adventure of living on a boat, surely a lifelong dream that includes halcyon days on the water, but undoubtedly also lonely, dark—and sometimes scary—nights at the docks. How does Herlong-Bodman find her balance, once she abandons the more-conventional days she has always known? How does one, living by herself, take in whole swaths of solitude and the unfamiliar? With trepidation but compassion and an open heart, we learn from this poet.

These poems are full of story. They show us the poet's devotion to the students in writing classes on the isolated barrier islands of South Carolina. They also take us along when she travels to the American Southwest, as well as to various cities in Europe and Asia. All these experiences—life aboard a boat and travels to landscapes and peoples unlike home—offer us a glimpse of how she tests her own determined resolve within and gives herself the chance to "take a leap, look deep inside."

For a woman who grew up on a family farm in the red hills of South Carolina, there is much new to experience, much to learn; and we as readers are fortunate enough to be privy to the lessons and insights. Along the way, these artfully conjured poems unfold their gifts, emotion by emotion, moment by moment. They introduce us to the dangers and mystery, as well as the beauty, of sailing and traveling alone. In "Sailing Single-Handed" comes this lesson:

> The thing you must learn is how to take the helm,
> anything to keep from drowning or being blown to sea—
>
> how to man the tiller when the pummeling begins,
> ignore leviathans that gleam and glare, dare to ride the swells

There is also caution to heed, when traveling in contemporary, unstable times—perhaps to places where governments are in the course of change and not always friendly, where there is unrest, as in "History 101": "Russian tanks painted / Pepto-Bismol pink / that summer after / the fall of the Berlin Wall." In contrast, the beauty of sights and sounds found everywhere the poet goes is described in this scene of the American Southwest in the poem "The Return." That beauty is easefully enhanced by the poet's own rhythms and repetitions:

>   before I hear the marrow-deep drum—
>   yellow birds, the Mayans, the Aztecs—
>   before the swaying, the singing, before
>
>   I drink rainwater from a gourd brought
>   across the Bering Strait, before I wrap
>   my arms around an early moon. Pray.

The scenic and historical abound, yes, but these are not postcard travel poems. Rather, they are poems that transport in deeper, more meaningful ways. The need for individuals to connect is a thematic given in Herlong-Bodman's work; the need for them to find words, or even gestures, in common—no matter what language each person speaks. It could be students along the fringes of the South Carolina coast speaking Gullah and trying to learn the grammar of classroom English; or on a bus somewhere near Prague, two women sharing bread without a word of common language between them; or Billy, the potter, in New Mexico, he with his mystery: "stories he knows / we do not understand"; or boys swimming up to the poet's boat off the coast of Turkey, speaking their own beautiful words in the poem "Found in Translation":

>   ... these boys
>   dripping wet, wide-eyed. You offer towels,
>   chocolate chip cookies, don't pretend
>   to understand their language, just let words fly
>   back and forth all afternoon.
>   *Gigek*. Flower
>   *Tabak*. Plate.
>   *Kozluk*. Glasses.

Introduction by Susan Laughter Meyers

At times, as the poet aptly shows us, the best connection is silence. In Tibet, for example, she intuitively turns to silence, even when it brings frustration, as it does when she tries— oh so hard, like a novice—to learn to meditate. These are the descriptive opening lines of the deeply resolute poem "Epiphany":

> Shuffling with pilgrims down dark corridors, air close with the smell
> of candle wax, incense,
>   wet wool, yak butter,
>
> a monk's incessant OMMMMM, bells ringing, wafting up
>   through golden frescoes, gods and spirits,
>
> I try to empty my mind, stay in the moment. Zen masters
> do it, medicine men, shaman. Why can't I?

No pretenses here. From the first lines of the first poem, we know that the words come from a searching and vulnerably honest heart. Yet the connections Herlong-Bodman seeks are not only between one person and another, but also between an individual and her landscape, the world around her—and in this poet's case, the sea. And perhaps most important, a connection with the self, the sort of understanding that comes from letting go of life's *shoulds* and *musts*, from society's often-artificial expectations. The sort of understanding that comes, as poet Galway Kinnell once said, "when one has lived a long time alone." All those dark nights, the quiet docks, have done their part to test Herlong-Bodman's resolve.

Along with beauty and danger and searching, what the poems ultimately add up to is joy: "and we sail out of ourselves." Ann Herlong-Bodman is onto something with her spirit of unmooring— this poet loosed far out, and deeply inward, into the unknown. Through her, we as readers are able to see the world with a keen eye, to delve into our own depths to find where the fears and hesitations lie. Prompted by her brave and magical odyssey so elegantly rendered, we might ask ourselves how far we're willing to go—to let our own spirits loose.

ONE

Trouble is

you have to stay awake when you sail offshore,
keep watch, the captain says,

watch for unmanned hulls, flotsam, rust
that clouds the mind.

Things that change us only change a fraction,
he warns. I squint, see only

phosphorescence, iridescence writing on a dark
and tumbling sea.

In such light, I see more clearly.

No need to check my compass to know
I'm shifting by degree, giving in without

a blink to places once denied. Makes me smile
when I decide to pay attention,

take a leap, look deep inside.

It's the lure

                      of the unknown that leads you astray,
my neighbor warns, fingers tracing
his voyage across wide and lonely seas.
If he fails, he will go down
in uncharted waters or waste away
on some forgotten shore. He's sailing single-handed,
moving forward, looking into himself
for answers, never veering off or pining
for the easy way, never foundering or wishing
for the white beyond the gray,
says he never regrets sailing into the wind,
never looks back at what might have been.

Is this the way he keeps up hope, leaves fear behind?

Fennel

Southern Coast, Turkey

Humps of bare mountains, rocks, a chalky-white road leading
nowhere, rusty fishing boats, baskets, red-braided officers

marching down the quay, arms stiff—*Come along*, they snap.
At least that's what we think they say. In the town square

beggars, spices, barrels of olives, pigeons.
An imam's prayer. Heat lightning. Sand

in my face. An old man, his face leathery
as the figs he sells, hands me fennel. I reach

for my travel book, page 192. *Fennel—
an offer of friendship*. He lies in the street to pray.

On Watch

What I will remember is not
that Venus was born of the sea, nor
Pygmalion sculpted from its Cypriot sand, not

that Saint Hilarion's Castle stands crumbling
under clouds—the saint's bones buried,
stolen in the night, transported to another land,

not even arms dealers with briefcases
and iPhones glancing sideways
from doorways in dingy cafes.

What I will remember is the freighter,
black, speeding toward the Middle East
rocket launchers, AK-47s,

my eyes blurring with images—children
laid out on bloody stretchers, women,
their arms empty—

the sea groaning, rumbling, howling
into a dark June night
sailing west in a summer gale.

Woman on a Hill

She's shaking her fists and sending curses
to the sky, *Meltimi, meltimi.*
Greek for *wind.* Or is it Turkish? Flower pots
overturned, geraniums scattered.
Elephant ear tumbling down the hillside.

Dark hair slips from the bun at her neck,
perspiration from her brow.
It takes time to catch my breath,
think of a word for *good morning.*
I help her clean. She invites me into rooms
breathing lavender and lemon oil,
hand-embroidered tapestries, handmade lace.

On the walls photographs—
a husband who works the sea,
three sons who follow, a daughter
who fled. Mixed loyalties,
invasions by the Venetians,
the hordes from across the Hellespont.
The Ottomans. The Luftwaffe. The Allies
who turned this island into blackened earth.

Should I have apologized or was it enough,
the way we sat all morning, no words,
just a language that runs through,
the two of us sipping tea. The way
I miss her starched white tablecloth, grape leaves
stuffed with lamb, pomegranates, Greek olives,
bread and jam—the Turkish kind.

Found in Translation

Water so calm here you can hardly
sail. Sailors call it *coasting*.
Blue sunlight. White goatskin tents.
Brown hills. Five boys

    waving armloads of purple and white bougainvillea
swim toward our boat. I imagine
all that speaks of conquest—
the Turkestani, the Gobie
out of Mongolia with horses on board.
The Corsicans. The Italians.

At the moment, however, are these boys
dripping wet, wide-eyed. We offer towels,
chocolate chip cookies, don't pretend
to understand their language, just let words fly
back and forth all afternoon.
Gigek. Flower
Tabak. Plate.
Kozluk. Glasses.
They give a test. I fail.

Later, as the Mediterranean
deepens blue to purple to black,
flames burst on the hillsides, families on holiday
cooking, passing down traditions and stories. Except
tonight the stories are about me, the teacher
who flunked the test— in my bunk practicing words—
words silent, drifting across water.

Looking for King Midas

Sails drooping, hardly moving, as if waiting for history
or myth to come down from the hills,
a sailboat drops anchor at the mouth of the River Pactolus.

Intricately carved rock tombs
plundered centuries ago.
A sandy river-bottom.
The boat captain rises, looks to the hills.
No discus throwers. No wrestlers' arms glistening
in the sun. Not an echo of Phrygian glory hanging in the air.

He dives. Maybe he's looking for treasure. Maybe he's
lured by spirits, or the memory of the girl
with the purple hair in the bar last night. For a while he swims
then breathes deep, dives to check the hull, when suddenly
in the shadow of his boat, marble columns quiver,
ancient sculptures line a street,
                              mosaic floors stare up

— hard to believe, and he thinks he hears moaning in the distance.
Sound waves traveling from all the way from Antalya? Vibrations
from afar? But no one here.
                              Someone crying?

Back in Antalya, he tells the bartender about
the sounds he heard, describes the mosaic floors,
the wine and feta he saw on a table. Cold
as war and greed and empire. Hard as precious metal.

Maybe his imagination is fueled by the ouzo
he's drinking or the tzatziki he bought
on the street. Maybe the sounds were spirits
escaping the river. No harm,

he guesses, just vibrations traveling out to sea,
but something seemed to be warning him . . .

and he can't say what exactly, but something
won't let go. And the bartender bends low, mumbles
under his breath, *It eats at you, man,*
chews and charms—his voice picking up—
until you got nothing left
but shadows
and a city at the bottom of the sea.

Taking Flight

Greek Islands

It is a gift, he says, and I
turn to stare at the stranger
and the necklace,
its stone as blue as the sky
I will not see today.
Flights canceled.
It will keep you safe, he says.
From what, I think.

I came . . . she not come . . .
please take, he says
and I lean forward
to let him place the necklace
at my throat, a blue-eyed charm
worn by the locals, its clasp
coaxing olive groves
and wine,
water the color of aubergine

and I embrace
the dream of strolling
through narrow streets
with the stranger, my face
to his, his hand sliding
down the curve of my back

as I straighten my skirt
and flip back my hair to peer
over the crowd, thank him.
But the stranger
is checking his iPhone,
waving goodbye, throwing kisses
while all around the sound

of the clasp lifts me
into a new light, the sky clearing,
passengers running,
and I'm standing
in the glow,
blocking the line at Starbucks.

TWO

Suite to Ashley Marina

Ashley Marina, Charleston, South Carolina

      1.

Fog eases close and gentles the water,
turns sailboats into markers
in some forgotten cemetery as I walk
down the docks between gravestones,
shoulders back, resolute. I, who
for a lifetime tied my wings
to red hills and clay, the smell of honeysuckle,
suddenly turned loose to listen
for the sirens at the edge of the continent.
Can you hear them?
In my dreams I repeat, *I do. I do,*
and I do in the morning hush as I rush to work,
head down. The docks beneath me
sway. A foghorn moans across the bay.

2.

Dog the hatches. Lash the sails.
A hurricane is setting itself loose
in far-away places. What to do
with plans undone, lips untouched,
words never spoken?
Not to mention leftover pasta,
promises broken. Look to the heavens?
Watch hope blow away while winds
rove, make history,
tangling boats as I
piece together an uneasy plea?
Suddenly a calm—the moon,
a halo of light, a miracle, I guess—
unless you believe miracles happen
for no reason at all.

3.

Bells ring. Sailors string lights, sing
to the wind. Fishermen, too. Plastic Santas—
red and green globes—wave and smirk
as if especially blessed in all this.
Across the street, a woman leans
at a hospital window, tubes tendrilling
from her nostrils. No one to hold her up.
Boaters hark to glory, birth, and kings.
Speakers blare "Joy to the World."
Stars drown. Deck hands raise glasses.
And after a two-mast ketch sails by
the woman appears again—someone
holding her up—the sky so clear I swear
I see angels streaking toward Bethlehem.

4.

Waves smack. Hatches freeze.
Docks crack and glaze over.
My neighbor's Donald Duck flag
hangs heavy-hearted from the top
of his mast. On such a morning when
the world hums of ebb and flow,
pushes back against everything that's
right and light, it's easy to wonder what
it would be like to feel mortality clotting,
the heart numb with the shock of it,
leave no footprint, no hymn to sing about,
no evidence of ever having been chosen—
disappear into thin ice.

5.

So what if I want impossible things.
Time in reverse, forward, backward
at the same time. Life foreign,
not like home but feels like home.
A heart that throbs, swells with
desire like a hunger budding into voice,
while never the song stops
but spreads always, not like a top
spinning aimlessly but soars like Venus
in Tannhauser, hands cupped,
calling with lust and longing
into life's deepest, darkest corridors.

6.

A man whose name we will
never know cries out for help.
Arms thrash, flail helplessly
against a current sweeping out to sea.
All night there's diving and darkening
search lights and sobbing
while not far away, a child opens Play Station
before he finishes his homework.
A wife waits for a husband to bring
his daily catch home for supper.
O things left undone. O world turned
purple. We stand on the dock
needing more than each other
to take us back where we were.

7.

On Jeff's boat, his girlfriend sunbathes topless.
Cigarette smoke curls from the bowsprit.
Jeff watches—they never talk. Boats nod
as if they approve. Workmen sing
"You Are My Sunshine." Fishermen cast
for whatever's out there. Reels whir, lines zing.
I'm back to the time my grandfather spent hours
teaching me how to push a rod forward
and let go the line just in time to send it flying.
Even now I can hear his voice, its timbre:
Could be something big out there.
You never know what might come around.
Each day a surprise, like living someone else's life.
Clouds unroll—pink, purple, Apollonian gold.

8.

If not for the traffic over the bridge, I could hear
drums beating in Africa. No rippling tide,
no childhood laughter. The back of my throat
thick until 3 a.m. when a breeze stirs through
corn stalks in the foothills, touches down
for a while in the Midlands, teases the coast.
How can I not lift my arms, think I can fly,
see those exotic drummers, hear the sirens,
and for no reason at all, I want to call
down the dock, beg others *come back*,
the sea is opening up its phosphorus hand,
but the wind dies down, ignores my plea,
as do all the others. They've tired of marina life
and left, they think, for something better.

The Art of Shucking an Oyster

. . . the ghost of history lies down with me,
rolls over, pins me beneath a heavy arm.
　　　　　—Natasha Trethewey

Long past sundown a tall man wearing yellow boots
heaves baskets from the back of his pickup truck.

Bonfire. Burlap. Dark men weave
in and out of shadows. Oysters roast.

Anticipation or the scent of it drifts
across the river.

Steam funnels up and into the longleaf pine,
up and up with the katydids.

When the oysters are ready,
the tall man wearing yellow boots wanders over

to the table where I stand, his thick arms announcing
he's not just any fisherman but an oysterman

who knows the Lowcountry heat,
its blowing rain, brackish waters, its estuaries.

I've never shucked an oyster, don't know how
to hold the knife, put pressure on the crusty shell
　　　　　　where the two halves meet.

He gives me gloves,

shows me how, guides my hand
to behold the rich and salty pouch.

You the new white teacher? He's speaking Gullah,
must ask me twice before I understand. Dare not

flinch. It's the first year of desegregation
on this speck of Southern soil, and I the token white,

snared like any animal in the glare of flame and truth.
Learnin' ain't enough, he says.

Thinkin' is what they need. Thinkin' can do it all.

Into the night we open shells as if by magic,
feast, outlast everyone in that season

of riots, overturned school buses, and protesters
hurling rocks, bottles, words. But this is the night

I remember—yellow boots, a man's smile,
his hands rough like a mollusk.

Over bridges and great spans

            of water to barrier islands
where, among parched hay
and used-up strawberry fields,
the old daydream machine
of making it rich in America
is slowly breaking down, I drive
after my regular school day

wondering why I think I can fix anything
but punctuation and syntax.
No matter. More students wait,
migrant workers—legal maybe,
maybe not—looking up as if I'm an angel

bringing promise bundled up in nouns and verbs
to men bent from planting seeds
in sand and women whose backs ache
from cleaning too many toilets.
What good is English wiped clean

of the motherland if it does not root them
someplace better, for the time being at least?
Tonight it's a concrete building
down a long sandy driveway set back
in scrub oak and pine—this one, a church.

Future Perfect

Another hurricane bears down
all the way from Africa

while students squeeze sounds
through cautious lips

as if they can save themselves
with twists and turns and tangled verbs

as if the day will come when they can swim
heads above water

sure their words won't slip away
leave them stranded

And I tell them

                    settle on a plan. Don't wait
all night, eyes cracked open, arms locked
around knees, yawning, wondering
what holds you to drowned dreams,
uncooked beans, the payment you
cannot make. Others may be wrapped
in flags, trapped in themselves, but
one morning you will wake to a light
intimate as breath, islands
rising in the distance. You've never
seen them before, never been there.
Who has not come into this world dragging dust?
You're afraid. Take heart. All of us are.

Gran's Funeral

Deacons float like a cloud down the aisle,
                                           black tie and tails,
top hats, crosses, white gloves, while up in the pulpit

Praise the Lord

shakes pews, hums through timbers,
echoes in the open casket.

It's your grandmother, Tabitha, lying there,
the gran you write about in the poems you read
in fourth-period on Fridays,

your gran who grew begonias
                                       in red clay pots,
snake plants in a white house set back in palmettos,
                                       sand swept clean.

Oh, Lord,
        Death comes at no particular time.

Three hymns, two scripture readings, a solo
by Deacon Davis and your friend, Tim, beside me,
                                       begins to squirm.

It's long after *Brown v. Brown* and here we are—
one white teacher and one white student
sitting down front with the Black church ladies,
all of us waiting for change like those
                               once bound in chains.

How much waiting is enough, your poems keep asking
and I don't have the answer, Tabitha. I don't know
how to make the world a better place, just know how
to make verbs and nouns agree

God's will be done

and the music starts again. The late afternoon sun
bursts through the door, and a multitude,

brothers, sisters, cousins, move up the aisle—
and there you are leading the procession.

It is well. It is well with my soul . . .

as a long wavy line of saintliness—spiced soap, hair gel,
and Evening in Paris—
                         makes its way to the cemetery

where they will find you under the shade of the tall pines,
and Tim and I, having come to the funeral
of your gran,
                     having waited this long,
will join you and your family in the circle—
as if standing with you, as if holding hands in a circle,
                     will ever be enough.

Third Birthday

Puffy white organdy, Mary Jane shoes,
cake and candles, a father who does not come.

Don't you move now, your gran warned.
Stand straight. He be here any time.

Whiff of lavender in the coolness
coming down the hall, sea-myrtle

along a sandy driveway, and a shape moving
in the great live oak, one lone white ibis

unfurling its wings. The hum of a boat
across the river. Ghost crabs popping

and scuttling in the pluff mud. Sounds
that will teach you how to sing the songs

you do not know, find the words.
O, love almost remembered. O, white ibis.

Morning Glory

Seventeen years your gran hung your sheets
on the line to dry. All your life she protected you,
prayed on her knees, whispered low,
Sweet Jesus, Lord have mercy
as she watched TV—police with water hoses,
drugstores in flames, looters in Walmart.

Today her yard was so covered in limbs and pine,
you missed class to sweep it clean, prune her morning glory.
Dead calm after a storm. That's what sorrow does, Tabitha.
Slows you down. Clears out debris.

May I come over tomorrow and help? Together
we will listen to the wind and imagine her
standing in the doorway as she did before she marched off
to protest or preach a sermon, shaking her finger,
Don't want no mess in this place.

Dolphin

It was barely light when I found you walking down the docks
with your gran's wide-brimmed straw hat, an ice bucket,
chicken necks wrapped in wax paper.

Fishermen already revving engines, drinking beer, crying out
                      to their Gulf Stream gods.

One dolphin leaping, flashing its body as if come to save you
as one came to lift Arion,
                      take him home to Corinth.

We watched while I told you the story of the poet kidnapped, then saved
                      to sing another day.

Once shackled, his lyre ruined, suddenly turned loose
                      from things he thought he'd lost.

I never let on that I knew you were skipping school, just like you
never let on. I was hoping you would find your way before the sun
                      grew white that day, and then the sun grew white,

waves glittered, and you said, *Everything will be fine again someday.*
You placed your hand over your heart. *I will write for her.*
                      We shook hands. A promise is a promise.

On Visiting the Site of a Massacre

South Carolina State College, Orangeburg, S.C..

Students stood where victims warmed hands
singing *We Shall Overcome.*

Guardsmen crouched. Rifles. Bayonets.
White-jawed muscles. Hate.

And when the song was over, grass red-tinged.
Bodies hope-spattered. Mud-soaked.

Three died that day. One mother fell to her knees,
soft-shaking. Hands hard-trembling. Kerosene flaming.

Lights went out.

What was gone was an only son, I told the class.
Fragile he always was, his mother said. Arm broke

chasing chickens in the yard. Only man
around the house. Body bent walking the line

white people draw . . .   The moment
seemed forever, but then you stood beside me.

Henry Smith is taller now, your voice strong, like your
grandmother's. *Taller still when it comes to dying.*

Be Careful What You Wish For

                                   Let's pretend the room is dark,
you on your blue bedspread dreaming, when your daddy
comes swaggering down the hall bringing presents.
Not here since Christmas, but he's come
to lead the singing on Easter, make your church thunder
with hallelujahs, rock with hosannas.

                                  Let's pretend he comes
to watch you in the senior play, you slip out front
to take a peek but he's not there. Not that you expect
a miracle, but let's say he appears in the second act,
your father's deep brown face reminding you
of yourself, how lonely you are.

                                       Then, one day
peeling peaches for a cobbler—crumbling sugar, flour,
more sugar in a bowl and smearing sweet salted butter
over everything, taking your time when a door slams, there he is,
smelling like Wild Turkey and Old Spice, you blinking
at white sharkskin and gold incisors, the loss, the years,

                                        when the knife leaves your hand,
clatters to the floor and Gran appears, lifting the hem of her apron,
fanning her face, speaking slow like she's from a branch
of some high-class family tree. *Every girl needs a daddy,*
but it's too late now. This girl done grown and walking in the light.
You can leave now. We don't need trouble.

                                   And your daddy steps back
before falling through the screen door, you leaning against the table,
thinking this is just pretend, but there's a knife on the floor,
your gran reaching for the Bible, shaking and praying,
peach juice running down your wrist.

THREE

Three Days Out, Somewhere in Middle America

And we yearn already
for sand, ocean,

and the Blue Ridge back home—
cedar, pine, leafy oak,

coming toward
us all around. What we see

is flatness—relentless, endless,
brown. The romance

we sought in this cross-country
driving trip dulled like old tonic

over Blue Sapphire gin. We've tired
of historical markers,

rabbit brush and cacti.
We leave the interstate

and side-trip into places like Secret Pass,
a town deformed, worn out.

Hope that started west but led to nothing.
We walk down dusty roads

to stand in wagon ruts
on the Oregon Trail, broken lives

roped off now. You're not to step
on dreams buried here.

All afternoon we drive in silence,
imagining a smoky saloon

at dusk with a mahogany bar,
brass foot rails, cowboys,

sheep men, miners mirrored
in glistening glass. Instead,

stark white boulders shine
like glass. We stop the car,

gaze as if half dreaming,
as if everything brown

deep inside will soon turn
green again, for which we will

drive all night under the crackling stars.

During a Visit to Bosque Redondo

                        I hand brochures
to students whose ancestors died under these
cottonwoods splintered beside the river, fields
turned into stubble, bushes dry in places,
swampy in others—thousands forced
to march here, thousands starved here.
No food. No firewood. No clean water.
They refuse to leave the bus, say
bad spirits here, and who can blame them?
If the truth doesn't matter, what does?
May we visit another time, geese circling
the willows in bright New Mexico sunshine,
learn the name—The Long Walk—feel the sorrow,
wounds winding through desert sand.

At Rushmore

Granite steams harsh in the mid-day sun
where a thousand bandanna-bikers
stare at stone turned into idols

like Ozymandias, once King of Kings, now
standing in the desert trunkless, unloved—
like the Colossus of Rhodes that lies
crumbled at the bottom of the sea

and the Agora, a rubble of broken marble. Here
people stare into air as if the world has yet
to see the likes of us.
Ask all these tattooed believers

rumbling their way to Sturgis,
stopping just long enough
to catch a glimpse of eternity.

Nobody Knows the Trouble

Miles and miles of powdery dunes where I go.
Not like the ocean where I come from
but sandstone, rock, and boys passing by

in wildly painted cars, music blaring,
teenage girls walking along the edge
of a past they do not know. Smoky eye makeup,
lips tattooed bright metallic.

What did I expect? A corn dance
to welcome tourists? Conch shells?
It's late when I find Pecos Pueblo where
they crowned Coronado with roses, this place

of splendor that came to nothing
when the white man swept this way
and medicine men were fooled.
This place I travel to see, this space

where women chanted, hushed their
fears and pounded grain at the grinding
stone. This place where dark vibrations
fill the air—their will and desire, their flame

and fire—as back home in slave cabins
where women sang of woe and wrongs,
and running through my head their words,
words to their songs running through my head.

The Return

In the time of tribal rituals and plum blossoms
young ones come home to dance, shake
conch shells, beads, chant with elders

in the sun-drenched square below—
the young who smell tomorrow at McDonalds,
sing songs to separate ways, sirens, horns.

Time and fissures have a way of upending
ceremonies, cottonwood trees,
river stories told around a fire.

She watches from her window, hair tied back
in the old style. Turquoise. Silver.
Pueblo walls rise behind her like a temple.

All day there's drumming and clapping,
and when dancers pack up for Albuquerque,
Tucson, or Vegas, she waves, at least nods

before she hears the marrow-deep drum beat
—yellow birds, the Mayans, the Aztecs—
before the swaying, the singing, before

she drinks rainwater from a gourd brought
across the Bering Strait, before she wraps
her arms around an early moon. Prays.

Woman with Gold in Her Hair

She's waving her blue-checkered apron and leaning
toward us, reaching out as we arrive for Sunday dinner.

Bless your heart, child. Just stand there.
*   Let me take a look at you.*

Hair sprinkled with gray now, she pulls me
into the kitchen, biscuits rising in the oven—

red tulips, white pitcher, still-hot strawberry jam—
quotes Milton or Shakespeare. Maybe Hawthorne,

I don't remember. But I remember the sun through
windows so bright I had to blink, and Uncle Fred

at the table, dressed as he always was—
in uniform, staring back into his war.

Today on the radio, two more soldiers killed in Afghanistan,
a drug bust in Albuquerque, and the summer haze

I'm driving through on the interstate—smoke
from an aging coal-fired plant—poison we all breathe

but I'm not really here, I'm driving into the light
of Aunt Goldie's kitchen, smelling her biscuits

and clinging to the memory of red hills, red dust
over fields of cotton plants, tender and young,

chopped and thinned when the moon's just right.

Standing at the Rio Grande Gorge

You would think you'd hear thrashing
as happens when tectonic plates move.
Roots, branches, pinion pine, sandstone
tossed about some thousand feet below.
At least hear the hissing sound
of phantom spirits rising
over craggy rock and angry thorns,
reminding you of grief and worry.

If not, you'd see blackened smoke
from some forgotten Hopi rite
billowing over sacred lands.
Instead where air is thin,
a sparrow flits. Eagles drift overhead,
bumblebees through scrubby brush.

No matter that earth could have ended,
swallowed up by atomic fission
down river in Los Alamos,
its secrets palpable as death itself.
This day the river flows tranquil
through the gorge, through tribal lands,
peaceful as a velvet ribbon
on its way to the Gulf of Mexico.

Prisoner of Earth

If only I could balance,
if only suspend in air

like a hawk
over desert land

where hollow dust
and hardness meet

or dance while
drummers beat

and wend
in ceaseless heat.

The idea here
is to overcome this

earth-colored sadness,
these bones worn smooth,

embrace the fevered wind,
the pounding feet,

crane to see what
comes next

before life flashes by
and I'm panicked.

One Summer Afternoon in Santa Fe

It could have been the wind
        sparkling leaves
        like weightless dancers
        leaping and pirouetting

or desire
        streaming into dwelling places
        touching bare shoulders
        as Loretto bells swayed,

but I think it was the Great Spirit
        making us think
        we could mend old habits,
        heal wounds—

all of us clapping, toasting, believing
        we were on the verge of something.

White people like me

go to watch
Billy, the potter,
mold pueblo dust
and yellowed earth
into wedding vases
and melon bowls
in his secret place
high above the prairie grass.

We drive for miles
over desert sand
and dry river beds
to earthen dwellings,
to fire and sage smoke
where he carves and circles.

He stares into the distance
toward Gallup
where his people
chanted the old songs—
his voice rising
and falling
in the ancient way,
as if he remembers
buffalo ghosting the prairie,
fields of corn,
squash in bloom,
drum song, night
vibrations on the kiva floor,
stories he knows
we do not understand.
Dare not ask.

FOUR

Epiphany

Shuffling with pilgrims down dark corridors, air close with the smell
of candle wax, incense,
                         wet wool, yak butter,

a monk's incessant OMMMMM, bells ringing, wafting up
                         through golden frescoes, gods and spirits,

I try to empty my mind, stay in the moment. Zen masters
do it, medicine men, shaman. Why can't I?

You could say my Uncle Howard, the reverend, could do it
when, in his stiff collar, he came to visit and preached us
                         to our knees.

Here no need to raise hands, kneel, or lie prostrate.
Prayer wheels. Beads.

Gifts of fruit and chocolate. Somewhere I will find the way,
                         leave bad karma behind.

Along the Lasha plateau, water sluices and streams.
Yaks graze on patches of green.
                         Crust of snow on mountain peaks.

Too high for trees. Only stone.
Stone fields. Stone bridges. Rivers of stone.

One lone stone house. Stone in my chest when I see her
                         standing at the door.

Prayer flags flutter.

Young ones peek from behind her skirts. She hands me
a cup of hot tea. My mind drifts to the me in me,
                              somewhere deep and dear,

the sky so clear I think I see, far up on the mountainside,
                              dandelions among the stones.

Passing Through

The sun disappears along this path.
Hummingbirds flash green then fly away like memories—

like the woman ahead, a husband who guides
and whispers as if reminding her

of a picnic, a blanket, crickets, one earring lost—
my memory, not hers.

I want to believe she remembers only the good,
that I, too, can hold at bay what's best forgotten.

Unkind things, scars, rains that cause the suffering,
tickets to somewhere else, rocks that make me stumble.

Thorn and brush on both sides,
the path narrowing. Uphill, uphill.

Is there no escape

                      like Danae, daughter of a king,
her fate sealed by Zeus, a shower of gold, a baby,
a chamber under the sea until a kindly fisherman
took them in? Her statue stands in scrub pine

on an island where a goat herder roams with those she loves best,
knows each by its weight, the curve of its withers,
bells tolling at their necks.

In Tibet, the crippled lay prostrate before the temple,
stones worn down, indifferent. This morning three
homeless men on the street as I walk to work.

Does life choose us or do we choose, all our tomorrows
undulating, floating just out of reach. Swallows
                                  ride the air. Gone.

Instructions for the Tourist

1.

Somewhere there's an old woman
scavenging for food.
Hold her hand as she stumbles
down a street or river bank.
Help her cut greens with a scythe
and stuff them in a pouch thrown
over her shoulder. Walk with her
through the fields or marshes
or desert hot sand
where announcements blared
before the invasion or the fall
or the last bloody coup.
Ask, *What did they tell you?*
She won't say.

2.

Roast sausages with Vlado
or Tarik or Yasin
who will explain again
why he was a Party member.
Smile when he tries
to repeat the vow he took
when he was young.
He will pretend
not to remember.

3.

Sit under the date palms
or bamboo or olive trees
with Anna.
Drink chai and listen
to her stories: how they
arrested her father
on trumped-up charges,
seized her home,
turned it into headquarters
for the jihadists or rebels,
how there are no records.
Burned, all burned, she will say.
Do not say, *I understand.*

History 101

*The struggle of man against power
is the struggle of memory against forgetting.*
—Milan Kundera

Russian tanks painted
Pepto-Bismol pink
that summer after
the fall of the Berlin Wall.
Dvorak in concert.
"Amazing Grace" on the corner.
Russian uniforms,
left by invaders

whose time had run out,
strung up
on makeshift clotheslines
high above the street, and you
jostling with freedom
on Wenceslas Square.
I gave you my copy of *A Farewell to Arms*.
You took me to your classroom.

She will help us with our English.
I spoke of Coleridge and his dreams,
tried to make sense of Eliot,
wrote Kafka's name on the board,

but when we heard footsteps
coming down the hall,
voices sharp and shrill,
your students' eyes grew cold.
You closed the door.
I erased the board.

Raising Two Glasses

*Mainly we sat staring at each other
across a barbed wire fence,*
he told me, said he tried to sleep

but kept dreaming of marsh grass,
shore birds, and a moon back home
so bright it kept him awake.

He imagined the soldier on the other side
who dreamed of swans dipping their long necks
in the steely waters under the Charles Bridge.

Both men cold as war itself.

Today they sit across a kitchen table.
Sunlight feathers through old lace curtains.
A map. Travel guides open.

Where? Here.

When? The same.

Smetana drifts in on a summer breeze;
couples stroll along the river. Laughter
floats up and up.

I cannot see which man
moves first, only arms that reach out,
come together, raise glasses.

Breaking Bread with a Stranger

An old woman climbs on the bus
as we roll toward Prague, her Moravian skirt
topped with starched white linen
embroidered with lilac and primrose,
pressed this morning
as she welcomed a new day
through the door in her kitchen.
When she sits beside me, I wonder
if she wants to learn English
at the language school where I teach.
Did her family flee when the Red Army
marched through the streets,
her sons interrogated, taken away
by the secret police? What was it like
to hide in the cellar numb with fear?
She opens a brown paper sack,
shares her bread, the last of her sausage.
The bus rolls past fields where women in black
bend and bend and bend
in a sea of yellow grain.
In the window I study my reflection—
lines deepening, a ribbon of gray
and the sneaking suspicion
that finally it comes to this, delicate
hand embroidery on starched white linen,
bread with a stranger, courage enough
to board whatever bus the world sends.

It's the Journey That Counts

Standing at the cockpit door, you told me,
                     Let's go. Let's sail beyond.
How far beyond, I asked as we glided through the harbor.
Rusty boats at anchor, lines tight like a noose.

Remember when the storm smacked us into a trough
and we jibed? You threw the tiller over and I
yanked at the mainsail.
                     I didn't know it would be so hard.

Remember the flash of lightning when I scrambled for a place
between here and there, and you asked,
                     Looking for a safe spot to blame someone else?

But the weather settled, we corrected course, and when a boat
passed with a woman at the helm of her own boat, you said,
                     I can see the girl she once was.

Once I swore I would leave no island untouched.
Once I wrote about catching stars.
                     Who's to say I won't stumble?

This is how it how it happens. One sail after another.
Life moves on and we sail out of ourselves. Hiss along
                     on someone else's compass course: drift
                           behind a boat blaring *Bolero.*

Sailing Single-Handed

The thing you must learn is how to take the helm,
anything to keep from drowning or being blown to sea—

how to man the tiller when the pummeling begins,
ignore leviathans that gleam and glare, dare to ride the swells,

although there are times when you need only press
your back against the cockpit seat to keep your balance,

horizons swaying up and down, right and left,
voices promising ports of call you've never seen before.

No one there to warn about the bars and shoals
that leave you high and dry, if not dead in the water.

When clouds hover and hurt howls like the wind itself,
it is the reefing and sheeting you must learn—

how to move through the queasy unknown alone, bend
chance your way, no matter the pitching and turning—

how to take the wind on the beam no matter the scars,
                         the bruises, the bloody nose—
how to stand calm, steer toward whatever's out there.

Notes

1. "On Visiting the Site of a Massacre" is based on the night heavily armed police and state patrol officers opened fire on unarmed Black students protesting around a bonfire on the campus of South Carolina State College, the carnage is known now as the Orangeburg Massacre. Three students died and twenty-seven others were seriously wounded on February 28,1968, three years before Kent State. The quotations from the mother are from *The Orangeburg Massacre*, by Jack Bass & Jack Nelson (Mercer University Press, 1984,1996).

2. In the poem "Third Birthday," "pluff," also spelled "plough," is a distinct and unpleasant smelling mud or silt found in the salt marshes and tidal waters along the Southeastern Coast.

3. "One Summer Afternoon in Santa Fe" is for Kathy and Greg.

Acknowledgments

I am exceedingly grateful for Susan Laughter Meyers, who wrote the generous introduction to this book just weeks before her untimely death. Susan's endless encouragement fostered my poetic life as well as that of many other poets, in addition to the poetic life of the entire Charleston community and both Carolinas. Her influence was wide and immeasurable. I am thankful for her incredible kindness, deep insight, and especially her friendship.

My thanks to The Poetry Society of South Carolina for its workshops, seminars, and awards that encouraged me along the way. My thanks also to the South Carolina Academy of Authors for its fellowship in creative nonfiction, which eventually led to this book.

I am grateful for the wider community of poets and the teachers who influenced my work at these conferences and workshops: Wildacres, Florida International University, University of New Mexico, Hub City Writing in Place, and the Press 53 Gathering of Poets in Winston-Salem.

A special thanks to the Palm Beach Poetry Festival and my ever-so-talented teachers there—Tracy K. Smith, Robert Wrigley, Carol Frost, and the late Thomas Lux—for their generosity. Special thanks also to Ginger Murchison and Nickole Brown for their insightful manuscript critiques and everlasting friendships. And to my fellow workshop participants, who helped shape many of these poems.

Thanks to Phebe Davidson and Cathy Smith Bowers, whose honesty and patience guided me through those early drafts.

To Press 53's Kevin Watson for selecting this book and for the respect he has given this work.

A million thanks to Jim Lundy and Monday Night Poetry and Music. To Libby Bernardin, Susan Finch Stevens, Rene Miles, Nancy Waters, Rose Marie Williams, Kathy Herlong, and Barbara Lasher who responded to individual poems, and to Candy Pou and her computer skills. Thanks also to my bridge partners who indulged me and to my local Dining for Women charity group who inspired me.

Thanks to all my family, especially my husband Robert, who always believed.

Ann Herlong-Bodman admits she is a recovering sailor who can't resist infusing her poetry with the majesty of wind and water and where there seems always to be someone traveling and looking for the next surprise. And surprises there are, whether it's a visit by teenagers swimming out to her boat along the Turkish coast or evenings on her boat in Ashley Marina in Charleston.

Herlong-Bodman's work has appeared in a variety of journals including *The South Carolina Review*, *Atlanta Review*, and *The Cortland Review*. Her poetry has won many awards from the Poetry Society of South Carolina including the 2017 Dubose and Dorothy Heyward Society Prize. She was nominated for the Best of the Net in 2016, and has published a travel book, a historical novel, and a poetry chapbook, *Pulled out of Sleep*.

She taught at the University of South Carolina School of Journalism and Mass Communications and at Lander University. She directed the Charleston Area Writing Project through the Charleston School District and after the Berlin wall came down, she taught in East Europe and directed programs for teachers of English under the auspices of the U.S. Department of State. She lives near Charleston, South Carolina.

Cover artist Dawn D. Surratt studied art at the University of North Carolina at Greensboro as a recipient of the Spencer Love Scholarship in Fine Art. She has exhibited her work throughout the Southeast and currently works as a freelance designer and artist. Her work has been published internationally in magazines, on book covers, and in print media. She lives on the beautiful Kerr Lake in northern North Carolina with her husband, one demanding cat, and a crazy Pembroke Welsh Corgi.

www.ingramcontent.com/pod-product-compliance
Lightning Source LLC
LaVergne TN
LVHW041344080426
835512LV00006B/608